Please return this book on or before the date shown above. To renew go to www.essex.gov.uk/libraries, ring 0345 603 7628 or go to any Essex library.

Essex County Council

Leaves of Love

Stories for ageing and dying well

Lucy Aykroyd

unbound

This edition first published in 2020

Unbound
T C Group, Level 1 Devonshire House, One Mayfair Place, London W1J
8AJ
www.unbound.com
All rights reserved

ISBN (eBook): 978-1-78965-088-4
ISBN (Paperback): 978-1-78965-087-7

Cover design by Mecob

Printed and bound in Great Britain by Clays Ltd, Elcograf S.p.A.

*In that abyss I saw how love held bound
Into one volume all the leaves whose flight
Is scattered through the universe around.*

– The Divine Comedy, Dante Alighieri

Contents

Super Patrons

Fiona Adamson
Carol Ann
Paul Ardern
Ali Avery
Rose Aykroyd
Susannah Aykroyd
Rosie Backhouse
Sarah Backhouse
Chris Barclay
Gill Bishop
Anya Bisset
Geirid Blunt
Sally Bolger
Elaine Bounds
Ruth Bradley
Louise Brown
Victoria Bryant
John Carr-Ellison
Katie Carr-Ellison
David and Heather Clark
Kate Clark
Libbet Cone
Elizabeth Cosgrove
Gail Davidson
Lily Done
Lynne Duncan
Marian Dunlea
Jenni Dutton
Hermione Elliott
Bryan Erasmus

Margaret-Jane Evans
Emma Evans-Freke
Aislinn Fawcett
Samantha Fern
Jolijn Fiddelaers
Anne L Forbes
Jean Forbes
Catrin Fowden
Trish Fuller
George
geraniumkiss
Kanada Elizabeth Gorla
Susan Greensmith
Mike Grenville
Mark Houghton-Brown
Norma Huntet
Vanessa Hurst
Tess Ingleby
Dru Jaeger
Liz Johnson
Judy
F. A. King
Moniczka Kowalczyk-Kroll
Rebecca Lambert
Gill Last
Lorraine & Christo
Claire Maitland
Christine Mayson
Jo Mcnamara
Denis Muirden

Natalie
Therese O'Driscoll
Sara Oakes
Gail Palmer
Nicky Parkinson
Lucy Parsons
Hilary Peppiette
Louise Pilditch
Bea Ramsay
Daniel Reaney
Desmond Reaney
Louise Reaney
Deborah Ritchie
Louise Scullion

Joyce Simard
Karell Sime
Jean Simpson
Joanna Still
Sophia Strang Steel
Virinia Strohm
Pam Sutherland
Gilly Kate Thirlwell
Rachel Thompsom
Una
Fiona Widdowson
Ron Wilson
Erica Wimbush
Janet Wimbush

Introduction

There is a thread you follow. It goes among
Things that change. But it doesn't change.
People wonder what you are pursuing.
You have to explain about the thread.
But it's hard for others to see.
While you hold it you can't get lost.
Tragedies happen; people get hurt
Or die; and you suffer and get old.
Nothing you do can stop time unfolding.
You don't ever let go of the thread.
– 'The Way It Is', William Stafford

We are all story carriers and storytellers. Each one of us has a bountiful basket of rare and extraordinary tales, most of which never see the light of day or a fireside tempting enough to share them.

It's a rare and beautiful thing to be able to spend one's days doing what you love. As a carer and end-of-life doula, I accompany others in their ageing and in their dying, an honour indeed.

I realised some time ago that I too have untold stories in my basket – stories that are powerful even in their simplicity. I offer them here, along with some reflections, in the hope they will inspire the carer in each one of us. Far from being morbid or dull, these glimpses into the experiences of others are reminders of the richness and opportunity often hidden within these transitions. Sometimes, we just need a little help to see it.

There is much we can celebrate in our later years: longevity is now an expectation but is yet to be fully exploited. We are inclined to focus on the negative aspects when in fact the laying down of responsibilities may open the door to new and exciting ways of being: a greater emphasis on spiritual matters, developing our creativity or the learning of new skills perhaps. Likewise, dying can be the 'crowning' of a life – something rarely understood.

Preparing for these later stages of life by exploring and discussing our options and making plans for our care is incredibly helpful and can make a huge difference to our attitude about the future. Standing on the threshold of our mortality and looking death in the eye does change things, perhaps forever. We may find we are already living the 'more time' that we would crave when given a terminal diagnosis and want to make the most of every single moment as never before; no more aimlessly wandering the shopping malls of life but seeking an active appreciation of each precious day.

Being available to help instigate these transformative moments is an important role in end-of-life care and an extraordinary experience to participate in.

It would be unrealistic to suggest, however, that ageing and dying do not also have their challenges. They will likely be accompanied by great sadness and the ache of loss. As a culture we have much to learn about deep listening and being present with another in their pain and sorrow, often overlooking the importance of expressing grief, both ours and that of those we accompany. It can also take courage. There is no road map; this is an unexplored landscape. But by accepting the inevitable and embracing the new, we may discover unexpected and wonderful aspects of ourselves and others, helping to make this a time of healing, completion and peace.

Storytelling is an ancient teacher, with the capacity to make sense of things bigger than ourselves. The stories offered here will, I hope, speak for themselves and encourage the carer in each of us to stretch out with fresh insight, yet never forgetting the wonderful wisdom we already have at our fingertips. We might be surprised as to what can happen when we add to this our creativity, compassion and humour. We all have something special to offer – the most important part of which is to turn up and share it.

I appreciate that I am reflecting in these pages the experiences of a rural life that is very different to most – however, these stories, unrecognisable as they are compared with their original format, relate to the humanity in all of us, regardless of circumstances.

I offer a deep bow of gratitude to those who lived these stories and to those who supported me every inch of the way in sharing them here. With their help I have done my best to keep the language simple, the ideas accessible and the words few.

May they serve you in the best way possible.

The Leaves of Love

The First Story Is My Own Story

I remember how my mother would hold me.
I would look up at her sometimes and see her weep.
I understand now what was happening.
Love so strong a force
It broke the cage...
– Mirabai (1498–1550)

When I was still a young woman my mother became unwell with what was then a mysterious illness. I wrote a small piece at the time to express how it felt accompanying her through her final weeks. It proved to be the start of my exploration into caring for ageing and dying people, the root of all the stories in this book from which the others sprung.

*

She lifts her hand as I descend the stairs. I turn my head and drink in the frail form propped in a sea of pillows and wave back. The role has reversed. Whose is the reassuring hand?

She has crumpled to the soft-edged beauty of a fading rose, one that can no longer walk, talk or hardly eat. Nearly every major watershed of dying has been breached.

Mum has never been afraid of dying. She has held it to be just the passing from one state to another – very simple. Now it is real. Now it is creeping closer and none of us knows what to expect.

The days of surrendering into the finality of the diagnosis have been and gone. She, who has known every aspect of her downland farm like her own body, can only access those folded sweeps on a special buggy, and her home in a wheelchair.

Conventional communication becomes impossible, replaced by a clumsy computer and a very laborious one-finger process. A small black machine swiftly follows – it talks for her, uttering long stilted sentences that sound as if we have a new male relative in the house! He talks of intimacies in a dominant bass that is incongruous in the frail woman who initiates them.

She is determined to sort out her affairs while she can. For her this means writing letters to those that she cares about and selecting readings for her funeral service. We sit round her bed like fledgling birds on the edge of the nest, singing out the chosen hymns. This comforts her.

Tempting morsels appear on trays. She is almost beyond eating but sometimes it adds structure and a measure to the day. The fragrance of jam, the familiarity of toast. Mostly a soft sponge dunked in water is enough. We need more than tea and toast but have no stomach for it.

'Now sweetheart, any visitors today?' We have passed through the valley of the frivolous and are on to whether a boiled sweet will help the mouth ulcers, and where can we get a commode? As the barriers of dignity fall away, we come to face the vulnerability that lies inside us all. Deep love and compassion emerge from such frailty.

Mum's attachment to this life is softening; she is retreating day by day, moment by moment. I lightly massage her feet, easing out each toe, restoring temporary warmth to their paleness, feeling her body soften under my gentle touch.

We are in the domain of soft clothing, light coverings and the fragrance of lavender oil. Heady flowers from the garden fill the room, as does abounding love. Oh, such tangible love.

A candle burns.

Inevitably, life goes on. I must go home to my children. 'See you soon darling,' I whisper, leaving my siblings to carry the load of pain and grief and, as it turns out, her dying.

When I return a few days later I sit at the end of the bed. My first dead body. I sit and gaze. I watch and breathe in this extraordinary moment. I appreciate from that moment that the body no more holds life than does the air we breathe. A container for it, yes, but a cage, never.

Following this experience, my life continued as a farmer's wife while I parented our children towards independence and, ultimately, freedom. I too then found myself alone, living in an old drovers' inn, way up in the hills of Aberdeenshire, until the day I saw an advert in the *Press and Journal* – the stalwart paper of the area, as anyone who has lived there will know.

Person required to offer companionship and an evening meal to an elderly lady, Friday, Saturday and Sunday evenings…

Two years later I would still be accompanying Marigold but, by that time, as she approached her dying. This was my first experience of being alongside someone as they made the transition from home to care home alongside the new territory of institutional living and increasing fragility. I soon realised I could sit in the fire with Marigold wherever it took us, and I would never shy away. I had found my perfect role in life.

A year or so after Marigold died, I was part of the first-ever cohort of students taken on by Hermione Elliot of the newly formed Living Well Dying Well. 'Are you happy to be one of our guinea pigs?' she asked, with a lift in her voice. Hermione, an ex-nurse with years of experience in palliative care, was in the process of creating a groundbreaking training – one of the forerunners teaching laypeople (and professionals) the fundamentals of being an end-of-life doula. I needed her and she needed me – a win-win. I was so excited to discover somewhere I could expand on the tentative steps I had taken with Marigold – a passion in the making.

Trundling down to Sussex from Scotland each month was quite some commitment, but it was there I learned the bones of being an end-of-life doula and some of the fleshed-out bits too; but the heart and soul I gleaned sitting in care homes, listening, watching, massaging hands, holding frail people in their weakest moments, singing lullabies and empowering ageing people to reach their full potential – while they still could. Fabulous work – though it never felt like work.

However, there were moments.

'I cannot give your card to my 85-year-old mother; she would not want to think she was dying!'

My focus began to move towards life-enhancing care – in those days, dying was very much a taboo subject so I had to go in by the side door. And I did – and it worked – and my heart broke open over and over – but as they say, hearts are meant to be broken. That is where the light gets in.

1. Love as a Healing Art

Vulnerable we are, like an infant.
We need each other's care
Or we will suffer.
– St Catherine of Sienna (1347–1380)

It's an interesting thing to notice what loving another means as we age. That soft, warm and sometimes exciting feeling that we experience when we are young usually mellows with the years, has a different flavour. Appearances matter less, the heart matters more.

The commitment to accompany and tend another, even when it's not pretty, is a wonderful expression of this love; to know that those who care for and about us will not shy away when things get tough, an extraordinary gift.

By listening and being attentive to what may seem like the tiny details of a person's life we can receive a valuable reminder to slow down, be actively present and sometimes to dig deep for patience. Possibly the nudge we need to become more than we ever thought we could be. I often feel I have gained more than I have given in these situations.

Leaving the comfort of our chair to hold a hand, stroke a brow or help with something out of our comfort zone indicates our willingness to bear witness and not to run away. I love to crouch down or kneel beside people – to take that risk with intimacy if, and only if, it feels right.

As we get older, the creeping conviction that we have done nothing useful or have little to contribute now is quite common; the natural degeneration of the body is somehow accompanied by a crumpling of confidence and self-esteem. An untimely and cruel duo, just when we are feeling at our most fragile and need to gather every shred of courage for what might lie ahead. No amount of positive affirmation completely overcomes this, but it does help.

If our care needs have moved us away from our familiar lives into a home, hospice or hospital, such reassurance is even more important. With our identity under threat, warmth and empathy from those around us make all the difference. As a

14

compassionate carer, it is impossible to overestimate the value of just turning up.

BETTY'S STORY – LOVE IN ACTION

Betty's dear face was always turned expectantly towards the door, eyes anxious and hands like fat little apples twisting the tartan blanket over her bony knees. The team in the care home usually remained at a distance when offering suggestions for lunch, and for very good reason – they were only too accustomed to her biting retorts and endless grumbles.

Betty was starving. Not for food, certainly, but for warmth and comfort in her heart. Over time I became attuned to what softened her resistance to being loved. Initially it was coming in close, holding her hand and offering positive affirmations. She let me gently brush her wisps of hair with long, slow strokes. Taking in a small bowl and lavender oil, I soaked her feet in warm water, massaging tenderly round each toe as I held her feet on a clean white towel in my lap. She would watch as if mesmerised.

I think it is important to mention here that there are times when it is easier for an outsider to fulfil this role – and is no reflection on the care already offered by relatives. A fresh face certainly helps but so also does the fact that we come without any history, any story that may hamper a family member from fulfilling the person's heart's desire or, similarly, overcoming someone's resistance to receiving care. I knew at the time that I was not physically able to care for my father in his dying due to our complex emotional history but have always been only too happy to tend other men when in my role as caregiver or doula.

Returning to Betty; over time she began to feel loved. We found poems she remembered and songs she enjoyed singing.

I pinned up beautiful images of animals and landscapes by her chair for her to gaze at. She never joined the others in the lounge, but more people now came to visit her. She continued to need frequent reminders of her worth and the sweetness of her life. Over time the lens through which she viewed the world began to shift. Her environment changed as she changed.

Increasingly disconnected from the land she loved, Betty found solace in wildlife films, being taken to the park, sitting outside with the sun on her face and listening to birdsong – these moments were all partners in her healing.

The team, with encouragement, noticed the change, and the atmosphere in Betty's room increasingly became one of welcome and reciprocity. With her heart softening, this venerable woman could be reunited with her family and community in a more wholesome way, while she still could.

REFLECTIONS ON BETTY'S STORY

Take a moment to remember how it feels to be vulnerable or ill. We have all been there; it can be a very lonely place. It is helpful to reflect on what was important to us in those moments.

Leave your own day at the door. Greeting each other with a presence that is clear and fresh enables us to be in the moment, without assumptions or conditioning. Within families we often bring old hurts or stories into our relationships. This new situation demands a new perspective – paving the way to forgiveness and love.

When faced with the unfamiliar our inclination can be to keep our distance. This may not be the most helpful way to make a connection. Coming in close, even kneeling beside someone and at eye level before gently taking a hand, somehow bridges a gap. It's comforting. However, as always, it is important to pay attention to body language – ours and theirs.

Simple actions such as brushing the hair or stroking the head can be calming, relaxing and beautiful examples of an empathetic response. Intimacies that were unimaginable in the past may become possible as age mellows us.

I often find that the people I visit are cold. Shivering is not conducive to relaxation and a sense of well-being. Wearing little more than a thin vest, polyester shirt and skimpy jersey (if they are lucky), clothing possibly suitable for an active life, is totally inadequate for ageing people and sedentary living.

Sometimes I wish I had a car full of rugs, cosy socks and robust underlayers ready to wrap around these chilly bodies. Warm blankets at night also give ease and comfort and enhance sleep. I am not sure why this aspect of care is so often overlooked.

Reminding people that they are fundamentally good, have lived a good life and are themselves loved is a very important thing. Many of us cannot hear enough of it! We are skilful at self-deprecation but are not primed to remember the generous and kind-hearted things we have done.

Finding something beautiful or that we admire about someone is always possible. It might just be the colour of their eyes – but first we must *look*. Familiarity often means that we cease to see.

2. Light-Touch Massage

A great consolation can be given to the very ill simply by touching their hands, looking into their eyes, gently massaging them, or holding them in your arms, or breathing gently in the same rhythm.

– Sogyal Rinpoche

How joyful it must be to know that someone will not turn away from our 'funny old feet', wrinkled face or life-twisted hands and will embrace us warts and all. Light-touch massage affirms these things. Our bodies and hearts respond to being firmly and kindly held, often feeling enriched, loved and replenished.

Many people say to me, 'Oh you don't want to touch my feet, they are so ugly.' But if we can, it is a beautiful gift. I appreciate that I am a particularly touchy-feely sort of person and usually arrive armed with nail clippers, lovely smelly creams and oils, hairbrushes, tweezers, good soap and a soft towel. However, this way of connecting is not for everyone. In fact, for some it is quite repulsive. We all have different things we can offer, and this just happens to be one of mine.

It is perfectly natural to feel hesitant about touching people, even more so when offering massage. Our cultural inhibitions and awareness of what is considered appropriate, especially with vulnerable people, have had a profound impact on how we approach these situations, sadly at times to the detriment of basic human connection. Non-medical touch is incredibly important: it is life enhancing, healing and healthful.

If we have been unwell, our whole being can feel quite battered by procedures, resistant to letting go into the hands of another – this is very normal. Yet with careful timing and discernment it can be the key to developing trust that is well worth the effort.

JT'S STORY – HOW MASSAGE CAN HELP

JT was not sure about all sorts of things in those early days, least of all about having his feet massaged. Some months later, he would have his socks off in a flash on hearing my voice in the corridor!

He was sitting, quiet and dapper in his tartan carpet slippers, when we first met; his family and I drank tea and ate delicious biscuits in his beautiful home. We spent a while getting to know each other. Progressing from casual visitor to someone offering care is a transition that must be sensitively handled, not rushed.

JT had been a railwayman and loved everything to do with trains. When he was in residential care he and I would head off on sunny days with his wheelchair to the museum by the station, where a model train tooted and hooted its way through a dusty, papier mâché countryside. Once outside he would take off his cap, lift his face to the sun and let the wind blow through his hair.

JT was a well-known figure in this little Scottish village. While he had lost his role in the world as he might have remembered it, gradually something new was emerging. We would push round all the streets, examining gardens, smelling roses, chatting to folk (and buying ice cream). Even the schoolchildren would wave. This was on good days.

On the not-so-good days, a foot massage calmed and soothed him. We would spend time together while his feet were soaking, singing a bit and talking about the happenings around him, the entire process gently bringing him home. I would slowly adjust the position of his chair as he relaxed, then gently work on his feet. Often, he would then sleep. Everyone could rest when JT rested.

REFLECTIONS ON JT'S STORY

Start slowly and simply. When I was introduced to JT, we just chatted, did simple jigsaws and wrote cards to his family. Over time, as he began to feel safe with me, and as his frailty increased, he was able to let me gently massage first his hands and then his feet.

Be clear about your intentions. Even as we age, without clarity we can get into a muddle and find ourselves in a situation that becomes inappropriate. Touch needs trust, and trust needs to be cultivated. We cannot assume that intimacy is always to be welcomed.

Explain exactly what you are doing and watch eyes and body language carefully to gauge how your actions are being received. Sometimes we can feel a tangible receptivity, at other times it is never going to be acceptable.

A gentle hand massage and manicure can give you the opportunity to be quietly together. Soaking the hands in warm water, working cream round each finger and nail bed, can be meditative and deeply relaxing for both men and women. Music may add to the atmosphere; however, simply holding a hand might be enough.

With a bowl of warm water to hand, and a little lavender oil, I often find that washing someone's face with a soft cloth or the edge of a towel – going gently and slowly round the eyes, nostrils, forehead and ears, then the mouth and jawline, before applying something that smells familiar, like Pond's Cold Cream – can be refreshing and restorative. We can all probably relate to that unpleasant, unwashed feeling – not a good place from which to face the world.

Having long and dirty fingernails can be really distressing for some people, yet often gets forgotten, especially in hospital, where time is at a premium.

For many people it is rare to have their feet really soaked and washed – showers are the norm in most residential establishments. I find that tending them is a gift I can offer that makes a significant difference. You can also learn a lot about overall health from examining the legs, ankles and feet, and not just about ulcers, corns and fungal infections. Swollen ankles may indicate issues with circulation and fluid retention.

As we work round the body in this way, we may notice other things too: poorly fitting dentures detract from the enjoyment of eating, flat batteries in hearing aids are unhelpful, as are aids that have fallen down the sides of the chair or have never left their box. Dirty glasses affect how we experience our surroundings. Unexpected or unusual confusion or wobbliness in walking may indicate a urine infection. We are not trying to be doctors here but paying attention at this time can help those who are.

Emotional well-being is sometimes harder to gauge. Discontentment, apathy or boredom can depend on so many things, so trying to ascertain what is really going on can be a challenge. The eyes and the voice are always good indicators.

3. Musical Interludes

Keep a green tree in your heart and perhaps
a singing bird will come.
– Anonymous

Singing is one of the most profoundly uplifting and healing of activities, whether alone, in a group or simply one to one. We can sing our way out of confusion, sing or hum when we can no longer speak and sometimes recall songs from our childhood when other memories have grown faint.

Most of us can sing something, even if it is only prayers, hymns or even nursery rhymes; nearly everyone has one or two songs tucked away in their memory bank. Once you find them, you are off. It can be surprising what a treasure trove some people carry inside them and how helpful it can be to creating depth and trust in a relationship.

It is not unusual for entire conversations to be sung when someone has lost the gift of speech after a stroke, relieving untold frustration, restoring autonomy and enhancing the whole experience of being cared for. I have found that singing together helps overcome all manner of difficulties. We can feel united when we sing, and in my experience, staff, visitors and friends frequently cannot resist joining in.

JAMES'S STORY – SINGING INTO FREEDOM

James's story is an example of how one gift, in this case music, can offer some compensation for the loss of another, in James's case, his sight. James became blind in his youth following an accident, yet successfully pursued a distinguished career as a university lecturer and writer, with many published papers to his name. His passion for music grew as these previous roles fell away and it then became the key to moments of great happiness as his confusion increased.

When James entered a care home he was unable to participate in most of the activities; the team seemed somewhat at a loss as to how to engage him. His days could be long. He spent most of his time in his chair, waiting for meals and visits from his attentive wife and loyal friends. James greeted each person with kindness and respect, receiving even a simple cup of tea with gratitude and delight. He appeared to need very little to make him happy.

He and I had sung together from the outset. The day I first visited him, he had his precious guitar by his side, and it was clear I had much to learn from him about improvisation. He taught me folk songs from his early life – I would look up others and teach them to him. Then we sang them, over and over. We gathered quite a repertoire. I took to singing as I walked along the corridor towards him – his head would lift, a smile spread over his face and he would join in.

James ached to get out into the sunshine and fresh air. Together we would walk slowly and carefully down by the river, him holding my arm and feeling the earth under his feet, listening to the water and the birds, and smelling the various fragrances on the air. And we sang. Singing was a lifeline, a way for him to celebrate his old life and make more sense of his new one. His guitar gradually gathered dust, but these shared moments filled the gap.

REFLECTIONS ON JAMES'S STORY

Ease your way into conversation about what music your friend might like – most people have loved at least one song. Take your time – music means different things to different people. Whistling, humming or just tapping out a rhythm on your knee might awaken a memory. Surprising insights emerge when you give space and time to let them.

The camaraderie of singing with others can lift a depleted state of mind. It is generally considered to be excellent for the memory, overall health and well-being, bringing people together like little else. Some people love to sing their way down memory lane with wartime favourites; others have more contemporary preferences and know all the words. Try to avoid making assumptions…

I take with me a small, portable CD player that has a good tone, a bag of recordings that cover many genres plus a handheld, remote-control gadget. I scour second-hand shops for new material (including DVDs) that will fill a gap or be appreciated by someone. It is helpful to build up a bit of a library.

It can happen that we are so overjoyed to have found a musician or genre that is appreciated, we forget to consider the other person's own sensibilities and leave it playing all morning. That has the potential to override any pleasure, perhaps forever. Be sensitive and consider what it might be like to be battered by sound, however lovely, for hours on end and unable to turn it off. (There are some excellent examples in the film *The Diving Bell and the Butterfly* about Jean-Dominique Bauby that illustrate this. See Reference Section.)

The TV is often the main 'entertainment' in some establishments. Silence is undervalued; we ourselves can be alarmed by it, preferring the rumble of the radio, TV or our personal favourite music on repeat. However, some people crave it – me for one. Older people have generally been more selective – they might be accustomed to listening to one thing, watching one programme and then turning it off. It's important to be attentive to this.

4. Food and Feasting

There's a kind of food not taken in through the mouth: bits of
knowing that nourish love.
– Rumi (1207–1273)

Food can be so much more than a way to sustain life. Food can be a celebration of being alive. Fresh food prepared with loving care and consideration nourishes many aspects of ourselves, some of which we may not even be aware of. It brings the outside inside, connects us to muddy soil, earthy smells and perhaps memories from childhood. We are never too old to eat peas straight from the pod!

When tending my terminally ill mother, her oldest friend would arrive with tiny offerings, beautifully presented on a pretty plate. Little scones with cream and jam, doll-sized sandwiches with the crusts off and little pots of homemade soup. She was aware, as many are not, that eating begins with the eyes. My mother latterly had a small and jaded appetite, along with a mouth full of ulcers, but could usually be tempted by these delicate gifts – even a few mouthfuls.

Mealtimes can be playful and fun, especially when shared.

GERALDINE'S STORY – THE TRANSFORMATIVE POWER OF SHARING FOOD

Geraldine's story is a constant reminder to me of the transformative power of sharing and preparing food together. She was a lacklustre soul bereft of true companionship since her husband died, yet her boys were determined she should remain at home up the glen, sure that this was best for her. However, her days seemed long and lonely, punctuated only by their visits and those of her carers. She remained compliant. However, her energy seemed depleted and her spirits were hard to rouse. I always felt sad when I visited Geraldine and somewhat frustrated about what positive change I could offer her.

Geraldine had lost all confidence in herself. Even going into the garden with its scattering of rabbits and grazing deer was an ordeal. Her quaint little house lay empty around her. She was confined by her lack of mobility to the kitchen and her bedroom.

The fridge was full of ready meals, sweet items and snacks but not much that was nourishing. Over time it was clear that Geraldine had very little interest in eating – a lonely routine that had to be got through, always on her own. She had almost given up, just grazing on what had been laid out on her side table. Her boys were busy, and not great cooks themselves, so any change would have had to be made by the already stretched carers.

We began, falteringly, to discuss what she enjoyed eating. We talked of favourite foods and why they were so delicious. What had been irresistible in the past, and what she had loved to cook. Then we made a list. The following week I shopped and brought the chosen items with me. We prepared everything together: carefully, slowly, peeling organic carrots, scraping organic new potatoes and laying fresh salmon in a dish. Having decided on the seasoning, we set these beautiful ingredients to cook. Then we laid the table: two places.

When the meal was ready, I put a rose in a glass, lit a candle and we sat together, appreciating what lay before us. With a small twinkle in her eye, Geraldine ate every scrap. I photographed the stages of preparation, the final feast and the triumphant Geraldine, before sending the pictures to her sons. We repeated this most weeks thereafter.

Something shifted in those brief interchanges. I released any expectations of radical change and came to appreciate that greater enjoyment of mealtimes was perhaps enough.

REFLECTIONS ON GERALDINE'S STORY

It is helpful to recognise that the food we were able to eat and enjoy in the past may change with age and frailty. Our capacity to eat will probably be less, and this highlights the importance of quality. Every mouthful should be nutritious. Even simple meals can be celebratory.

Fresh and tasty food is fundamental. I have sat with a friend in a care home, who was sawing hopefully through a grey, dry, 'cardboard' square of fish that hadn't seen the sea in a long time. It was served with cold chips. Hardly tempting to a jaded appetite or, in fact, any appetite at all.

Many people have cooked enthusiastically for family and friends at some stage in their life – they will have a knowledge of, and maybe even a passion for, something, whether it be baking or roast dinners. It's an interesting journey to uncover that talent. For some, it can be a relief not to be involved with the process of food preparation. For others, a lasting sadness.

Be cautious with snacks; too many and the carefully tended appetite will be unable to enjoy any delicacy, however beautifully prepared or presented. Of course, there may come a time when all any of us feel like is cake, chips, boiled sweets or ice cream – or even nothing at all: so be it. A friend of mine's mother lived largely on the case of lager that lived under her bed.

Ready meals have their place, and some are better than others. However, well-prepared home-cooked food takes some beating, especially when it smells delicious and is presented nicely. Tempting the senses is vital.

Medication can reduce both the appetite and the enjoyment of meals, so start with tiny portions. There is nothing worse than being faced with a plateful of food more suitable for a teenager. Tiny is best.

Eating together turns food into a feast. Yet it's not easy being observed. There are occasions when it is preferable to eat alone, so be sensitive to that. Our mouth muscles may be slack, swallowing difficult or we struggle with mouth ulcers; then it's more restful to eat quietly, without feeling self-conscious.

5. Nature as Healer

I only went out for a walk, and finally concluded to stay out
until sundown
for in going out, I found, I was really going in.
– John Muir

Many of us are far removed from nature, its throbbing pulse and exquisite rhythm. I am fortunate enough to live on a shoreline. The ebb and flow of tides are with me all the time. I experience deep darkness, the essence of seasons and the opportunity to be immersed in woodland and wild weather – states of perpetual transformation. Birth, life and death all exquisitely enacted in and around me.

It is becoming ever more apparent that, without some aspect of the natural world in our lives, we can feel that something fundamental is missing, and that there is an inner rumble of discontent that will not go away. As green spaces retreat, so can contentment. Perhaps we are eating, sleeping and functioning as normal yet one day get taken by surprise when out in the woods, or when on the land somewhere we have this irrepressible longing to throw ourselves down in the long grass or walk barefoot on warm earth. Maybe we see a beautiful photo of a river or landscape and find ourselves welling up with tears... it can be as if the heart is shaken awake, the spirit come alive.

That nature could wish to be in relationship with us as we are with it may seem very strange. That the planet on which we live is vitally alive and not just a sentient being with no voice could be quite baffling. (And possibly inconvenient when you think how we treat her.) Imagine for a moment how joyful she might feel if we re-engage and walk out each day with our eyes and ears unveiled, and our heart open to experiencing something new.

The pain of severance from the land can be a particularly unsettling aspect of growing older, especially for those for whom the mystery of nature and knowledge of birds, trees and the cycles of the seasons were part of normal life. A truly poignant and unrecognised loss. Disconnected from the familiarity of dewy grass, the star-spangled sky or soil rubbed between dirty fingers – this may seem very final if there is no one who recognises these feelings.

It is clearly documented that spending time in wild spaces has a profound effect on children, teenagers who have difficulties or prisoners who are being rehabilitated. Hence the emergence of forest schools, wild camps and prison farms. However, we do not seem to appreciate the enormous value of wild spaces in quite the same way as we age.

Finding opportunities to engage older people or those who are very sick with the natural world can seem insurmountable, especially when they are tucked away at home or in bed. However, there are simple and beautiful things we can do. They may just take a bit of ingenuity or imagination.

One lovely option is to tantalise the primary senses by bringing nature in all its rawness inside: earthy smells, crunchy sounds, recordings of birdsong or posies of dew-fresh flowers. Small and tender moments can be really reassuring and elicit a smile. They also carry memories and stories that lead on to other possibilities. Healing takes many forms.

PAUL'S STORY – ONE MOMENT, TWO MOMENTS

Paul, a Quaker, spent his early life on a Scottish island. On returning to the mainland, he left part of his heart behind. We shared this passion for Scotland. He loved the land and often talked about those early years on his grandparents' farm with great nostalgia.

Tragically, the dementia from which Paul suffered proved to be particularly cruel and reduced him latterly to a very sick and distressed man. I massaged his feet and tended him gently, always paying attention to those tiny details, such as clean hands and tidy nails, which mattered so much to him.

We would also sing. We had always sung together, the 'Skye

Boat Song' and 'Loch Lomond' being his favourites. They touched something deep inside him which had slipped under the barricade of his illness. Even in his frailty, curled in a foetal position in a sea of pillows, he would suddenly rouse himself, take a big breath and join me, belting out a few lines in a surprisingly resonant bass. Nurses would stop and peer amazed round the door. Tears frequently flowed.

Around this time, I was in Scotland, near Golspie. The sun rose pink over the sea to the chorus of lark, curlew and oystercatcher. Heron and cormorant stalked the shoreline. I recorded a small audio clip of this on my phone.

On returning to Paul a few weeks later, I found him face to the wall, still curled in a foetal position but retreating further into a tragic state of resignation. I felt heartbroken witnessing him like this. Instinctively, I came in close, laid my hands on his shoulder and hip bone and crooned to him, as I would to a baby or sick child. We sat together for a while, me listening carefully to any negative response from him or a responsive softening to my touch that might indicate how to proceed. Finally, I reached into my pocket and took out the recording from the beach at Golspie. Laying the phone close to his ear, I played him the recording of lark, curlew and oystercatcher – the soft sweep of waves filled his little room. Tears oozed from under his closed lids. 'Heaven,' he murmured. Very different to the 'no one should have to go through this' refrain which was more common.

It is impossible always to get it right, and sometimes one gets it badly wrong. However, there can be moments when everything appears to come together and, for a blink, all is well. This moment was one of those. It interspersed many others when just sitting quietly, helping him drink, sliding a milk chocolate between his lips or sponging his face with a fresh, warm flannel was enough. Resting with him, reading a paper, holding his hand or knitting beside him were peaceful moments that reminded Paul that he was loved, not alone, not abandoned.

Paul appeared to really appreciate the constancy of his closest friends as he wrestled with his illness. The power of presence, and the reassurance of being recognised for who we truly are, are immeasurable. We can always offer those. Despite him taking quite a cocktail of calming medication, I could usually find Paul somewhere – it was just a case of discovering the key.

Touch was one. Imagine not being hugged or held. It is a tragedy that many of us wait until we are dying before being cradled once again as a child and, even then, may wait in vain. Paul's little body would settle and sigh when held – a deep letting go and he could just *be*. So fundamental.

Paul's story is a great reminder that we must never give up on anyone.

REFLECTIONS ON PAUL'S STORY

Reawaken the senses by touching, feeling, smelling and listening. Even a butterfly on the curtain or a snail on the windowsill is a joy to witness and an opportunity for conversation and connection.

Being outside in a garden or sitting under a tree often makes a welcome change, even for a very short time. When warmly wrapped up, the caress of the breeze in our hair, the sun on our face or our bare toes on the grass is unimaginably wonderful; even more so when our normal life has radically changed. Likewise, to be taken out under the stars, to experience darkness again or watch a flaming sunset is a precious gift.

A well-maintained bird table close to the window offers the opportunity to gaze with purpose – like a silent movie. It is possible to engage just as much as one is able. Or not at all.

Developing a relationship with a tree or plant in the garden, especially when that connection is shared with another, can be a wonder – the changing colours of leaves, the dripping of rain or the movement of creatures who inhabit the tree community. One of the joys of ageing is that, as the outer world contracts, we can pay greater attention to exquisite details.

Keep it simple: a sprig of newly emerging beech leaves in all their vibrant greenness, planting snowdrops in a pot or bringing a fresh apple to share can all rekindle comfort and connections that may not be reached in any other way. Cut the apple together, watch the juice ooze, smell it and count the pips. Perhaps it is possible to bring some chicks in a box, a puppy, lamb or even a sheet of honeycomb. So much richness to share.

Think of photographs that inspire you, poems you enjoy or passages of prose that might be appropriate. Take them with you; try them out. It's worth experimenting to see what works best. I, for example, would only read books to my children that contained pictures that I liked. It is the same here: if you love it, you are more likely to bring passion to what you offer.

Slipping into confusion must be so scary. It is deeply reassuring to have someone in our lives who will not turn away when we reveal the depth of our suffering, anger or fear. However, as a caregiver, we may then find ourselves unexpectedly catapulted into the role of parent, whatever our age. Another new experience.

6. Creative Imagination

I am enough of an artist to draw freely upon my imagination.
Imagination is more important than knowledge. Knowledge is
limited. Imagination encircles the world.
– Albert Einstein

The imagination is a powerful force and one we can easily underestimate. We have only to think of cutting a lemon in half to salivate or remember something beautiful to smile. The imagination can take us anywhere – back and forth in time, to ecstasy and pain and on again to create the previously unimagined. We can walk in a loved garden, smell seaweed on a shoreline or rest by a lake, any time we desire. We can also envisage a healing, a wholeness or a world transformed.

The confines of a bed can be what it takes to discover this joy and be set free to fly. It's not a bad idea to cultivate this freedom; we do not know when it will be needed. Ruth, who is mentioned in this book elsewhere, reminded us in our yoga practice to breathe into different parts of our body, to envisage an expansive moment before we did it and enlist the power of the imagination to effect positive change in our lives.

My mother also taught me about the power of the imagination.

One of her stories was of visiting a bed-bound friend who adored her garden and missed being able to wander and work there. Allowing the quiet of the bedroom to envelop them, my mother frequently guided her on an imaginary journey down the stairs and into the sunlit garden. There they examined each plant and smelled each rose until it was time to return, back up the stairs and into bed. The friend did in time retrace those steps in her body and lived a full life once more. Who knows how much the imagination participated in this healing?

MARIGOLD'S STORY – THE IMAGINAL WORLD

Marigold was in her sitting room, peacefully reading, when I met her. The window to her garden was open, the rustling of poplar leaves filtered into the silence. She cocked her head and looked at me. I was reminded instantly of my mother.

Mum was wrestling with a devastating terminal illness when my own children were young; I was living far away and could not be with her as I would have liked. The time I was to spend with Marigold was one of those rare opportunities to relive an experience in a positive way, such as I had been unable to do in the past – a second chance to tend and love her by proxy.

When Marigold moved into residential care it was hard for her – she adored her freedom and she adored her home but sometimes life dictates that we let go of what we hold most dear and she did just that, and with amazing grace. Her family made the transition as seamless as possible and created a welcoming, homely space of her room, yet she still loved to escape. And escape we did.

We entered the magical world of our combined imaginations: telling stories and remembering places and experiences that held strong memories. With her leading the way, we boarded boats, galloped stubble fields and visited wild islands, all in an afternoon. Marigold appeared to love these adventures. I came to understand that the body doesn't really know the difference between the imagination and reality.

In addition to our imaginary journeys, we shared many other happy times. The core of us rarely changes – we continue to love what we have always loved, even as we age. Marigold's lifeline was being creative, whether out in nature or sitting by a fire. So, with that in mind, we took drives to much-loved places where she could draw and went to a small pub nearby that had a fire and served her favourite liver and bacon. I would also take her to my home in the hills where, like a small bird, she would trot through to the sitting room and, tucked in with cushions and rugs, sit and gaze tirelessly at the leaping flames in the grate, apparently entranced.

And then she cooked. We all carry an assemblage of skills that we have garnered over a lifetime, but I think bread-making was a new one for Marigold. Her eyes glittered with joy as she tossed flour in the air and kneaded great gobs of dough – I have the photograph still. Christmas puddings came next.

Marigold fully understood the need for giving as well as receiving, something so easy to forget when in the caring role. On Marigold's insistence we went most weeks to the local shop, from which she would emerge with armfuls of blooms. The following days were spent sorting the little florist's shop in her bathroom (the toilet making a great vase!) until finally pretty bouquets were distributed with a cheeky smile to her carers. I learned so much from her about what really matters when on the receiving end of care.

I accompanied Marigold when she made her final journey; holding her, singing with her, reading to her and loving her, an experience that has informed my life and my work ever since. She was always clear whether what I offered was to her liking or when I had gone a step too far: 'That's quite enough of that, Lucy!' More valuable learnings from a wonderful teacher.

REFLECTIONS ON MARIGOLD'S STORY

By extending our own creative imagination we can cultivate fresh or forgotten moments of happiness for those we accompany. It's a thrill to find we can learn or get excited by something new, even when we feel we are 'past it'.

Transplanting one's life into the confines of a care home can be a terrible shock. It can also be a relief if life at home has become a struggle. Either way there are sacrifices and compromises, some of which are easier to cope with than others. Having regular visitors who remind you of the other you, the you that you identify with, is incredibly helpful.

Losing our identity, our old role in the world, can be another shock. Being 'idle', an entirely new experience. Most people have had active lives, even in retirement, and have great expertise tucked away. Gardeners, bakers, busy grandparents and very competent householders. When accompanying another at this stage of life we can draw on these experiences and use them to help make life interesting and fun once more. One caregiver where I worked commented, on returning from the funeral of a resident, that she had no idea that he had lived such an interesting life...

Feeling we belong, feeling we are known and recognised, is an important part of being human, as is being able to 'live the normal'.

Marigold loved to read and, latterly, to be read to, especially from familiar books associated with her childhood. She knew many poems and longer passages by heart, reciting Longfellow and Shakespeare right up to the end of her life.

The imagination is a BIG fire. Light it! If we are always confined by the known, nothing fresh will grow.

7. Sorting and Tidying: How the Familiar Can Help

Tenderly, I now touch all things,
knowing one day we will part.
– St John of the Cross (1542–1592)

There comes a time for some of us when it is hard to settle. Illness may have taken a hold, our memory is failing or life is just plain difficult. Some dementias can be very debilitating, will probably be horrible to experience and are certainly distressing to witness. At these times, rather than retreating, it is helpful for all concerned to have some fresh ideas to hand. In my experience, engaging in familiar activities can be useful, triggering a happy memory which renders them safe and acceptable, giving moments of calm and purpose.

In residential care, having a quiet area set aside where these sorts of projects are carefully laid out in an appealing way gives people the freedom to choose what they would like to do, always ensuring that encouragement and support are available. Even when not overwhelmed by dementia, boredom and apathy are rife in many establishments, so it is important to rekindle old skills and restore self-esteem whenever possible.

Carers, although extraordinarily capable in their field, are often lost for ideas as to what to do with those in their care when time allows. Maybe some of the suggestions mentioned below will help.

MARTIN'S STORY – CREATING ORDER

Martin's story is a great reminder to me of what is possible within the simplicity of everyday tasks.

Always robustly dressed in country clothes and with a red and white spotted hankie around his neck, Martin was somewhat distracted even when I first met him. He and his wife lived deep in wild countryside, down a rough old track that led into a copybook farmyard, with chickens and ducks scattering stray straws. Horses stamped in the stables and the sun always seemed to be shining.

It took a while to gather a picture of what would make

life easier for Martin and his family. He was a man of the land, always surrounded by horses, livestock and children – we would go outside as much as possible and sit under a tree, surrounded by pecking hens and lounging dogs. Moving the parasol to shade him from the sun, I would read to him, sing with him and sometimes gather items from the garden to show him.

On other days, Martin would just sit waiting for something to happen, his eyes straining to see who might be arriving in the yard. He could be quite vocal as he waited. After a while, it was important to find an alternative that would give him some moments of peace.

Following the example of his remarkable wife, we humoured Martin, laughed with him and never contradicted him. This approach, along with soaking his feet in almost-hot water (no tepid for him) and lots of slow massaging of his feet, legs and hands, continued to be helpful until we got to precisely 3.30 in the afternoon, when a new level of confusion would kick in. You could set your clock by it. No one could fully understand the reason for this instant shift, so we just worked with it as best we could.

I would lay out boxes of cutlery or old tools on the scrubbed kitchen table. Martin could be quite absorbed by polishing and sorting for extended periods of time, before suddenly pushing back his chair and moving on to something else.

Home was a place which, for Martin, was full of familiar routines and rich with memories of reading with his granddaughter and loudly singing long-remembered songs as the sun streamed through the windows of his room. There came a point, however, when even our best endeavours were not enough to distract Martin, but until then we helped him make the most of every moment of his life at home.

REFLECTIONS ON MARTIN'S STORY

Here are some ideas to consider that have proved helpful to me in the past.

A box of cutlery with cloths to polish each item in turn can be absorbing and is easy to provide. These items can also be sorted, over and over, into compartments or laid out in bundles.

A box of buttons on a tray can be engaging as together you sort them by colour, shape or function, perhaps into different jars or baskets or threaded onto laces.

Shoe-cleaning holds the attention of some people, especially for those for whom this was a regular activity. The smell of polish, the traditional brushes and yellow duster all help.

Kneading bread dough is very satisfying – dough is very forgiving and can be pummelled mercilessly.

It must be very strange to be deprived of familiar tasks. I have found that having a basket of laundry to fold, a stack of little yellow dusters and old-fashioned polish to hand, knitting to unravel or skeins of wool to roll are all useful.

Polishing brass is good fun too or sorting a box of old metal items, such as keys, bolts and old harnesses with buckles.

It is possible to buy very lifelike dolls that give great comfort to many a frustrated grandparent; they can be nursed, dressed and repeatedly swaddled in pieces of blanket. See link in Reference Section.

Sensory bags, 'feely bags' and lavender bags offer loads of potential.

Clay is another material that is grounding and pleasing to use. There are many varieties to choose from, which range from the 'real thing' (can be messy) to quick-drying and cleaner brands. Even playdough works well. A good craft shop should be able to help.

Put a tray with little flowerpots and a bag of compost on a table or in the garden – large seeds such as courgette, marigold and marrow can be easily planted in the soil. Daily watering creates a pleasing routine.

Planting bulbs is also gratifying; they are easy to handle and make useful gifts.

Feeding chickens, an aviary of birds or fish in a tank is great for enhancing connection to the natural world. So is measuring out dog food or filling peanut feeders.

Libraries offer the wonderful service of supplying books to care homes. It is possible to specify the type of books required so that large-print and coffee-table books with lots of pictures of wildlife can be accessed easily. They can be changed regularly.

Games and puzzles are great, but they need to be kept up to date and be complete. Most jigsaws have very small pieces, but it is possible to get extra large ones which make them simpler to do. Left out on a table, everyone can engage with them in a companionable way.

Nature films, on repeat and with the sound down, can be played on the TV or the wall of a room. There is something about gazing at animals that is very soothing. Simple films without a story also work well, as does classical music that calms the soul – try old favourites such as *The King and I*, *Oklahoma* or *The Sound of Music*. Be sure to play what the person you are with likes rather than your own personal preference. Of course, if they are the same that is a great bonus.

Being read to is very restful. *Cider with Rosie* by Laurie Lee has proved very useful for me. It touches a time in history that is familiar for many and resonates.

8. The Importance of Community

Relationship is to all things, to nature – the birds, the rocks, to
everything around us and above us – to the clouds, the stars and
to the blue sky. All existence is relationship. Without it you
cannot live.
– Krishnamurti (1895–1986)

Growing old in our culture is not always a pleasant experience. It is not unusual for people to feel quite fearful, living out a life that they never imagined for themselves, a life that based its trust in a medical profession that has run out of answers. Admittedly, the sheer practicality of tending an ever-increasing number of ageing individuals is a massive task.

Not surprisingly, we can find ourselves lost in a system of 'time pressures' and 'outcomes', dependent on medication and routine visits from time-restricted carers. In the centre of all this are frail, fragile humans, often without a voice or the strength to express what they need. In many instances this is changing, but I feel we still need to remain attentive.

When, perhaps as late as midlife, we witness the irreversible ageing or death of someone we love it can be truly shocking. Concealing our elders has resulted in our young people rarely being exposed to the beauty of ageing and the possibilities around dying. Traditionally, growing old in a village was different. We may have lived on bread and tea and become quite grubby, but we were part of a family, part of a community, and youngsters grew up alongside it all; the good and the difficult. It was a normal part of life. Family cared for family, sometimes for better and sometimes for worse but it was all there, in plain sight. We are not so easily frightened by what we know. Now we are often ill equipped emotionally, physically and spiritually when faced with what is a normal transition.

Away from our familiar home environment we can feel dislodged, invisible and superfluous, believing that no one cares if we were the Mayor of London, made the best oatcakes in the village, or grew the most fragrant roses; just dissolving into waiting for the tea trolley or a toilet break. As neighbours, caregivers, friends and companions we can contribute enormously to someone's sense of autonomy and belonging.

Lucy Aykroyd

PETER'S STORY – EXPECT THE UNEXPECTED

Peter lived at home on his farm, largely thanks to the loving attention he received from his sons and visits from friends in the village. A stalwart, traditional farmer, with neighbours who beat a regular path to his door for true North-East hospitality: village news, a 'dram' and a 'fancy piece' (usually shortbread, preferably home made). Failing the dram, tea was obligatory.

Peter's ruddy cheeks, ready humour and bright eyes spoke of the hours he had spent on this tough old bit of land where the winters are harsh, summers sometimes non-existent and every day revolves around the elements. There is nothing this extraordinary man didn't know about stock, crops and the price of barley. He was also a keen observer of the wildlife around him: no small bird, migrating goose, vole or weasel escaped his eye.

His sons were remarkable in supporting his continued involvement on the farm as he aged: inspecting the cattle from the vantage point of the jeep in the mornings, feeding the hens and including him in all the daily happenings. He continued to cook their tea each night and they, in turn, appreciated his efforts.

On one visit, he and I talked of music – not a subject I had expected him to enjoy. Peter remembered two songs he had always loved. One, 'The Ugly Duckling', the other, 'Just One More Time' by Gracie Fields.

When I next visited Peter, I had found those songs on Spotify and saved them offline. When I told him about this, his eyes opened wide with amazement – such newfangled technology being quite outside his experience. From the depths of my phone, first Gracie Fields and then 'The Ugly Duckling' sang out. He listened to the first song with his head cocked on one side, but when it came to the second, tears streamed down his face. I held his hand. When it was over, he was quite taken aback. He recovered himself and we talked gently about where those tears had come from. After a while I offered to play the songs again. Once more, he was deeply moved.

A touching shared moment, so simple to execute. No one was more surprised about how Peter and I had spent the afternoon than his sons, or what musical memories we had uncovered. I will never forget the light in his eye as I left him that day.

It's so easy to stay away when things get difficult. 'They won't know me', 'I don't know what to say', 'I will go next week'. That next week may never come. Quite simply, pocketing our knitting and a book of poetry or a recording of birdsong is often all it takes; and half an hour. It will never be wasted.

We owe it to ourselves and our communities to support those who look after ageing friends or dependents at home; the younger generation need to bear witness. They learn about love this way.

REFLECTIONS ON PETER'S STORY

Dare to be open to whatever presents itself when you visit someone, even if you know them well. There may be a surprise in store!

Remaining at home as we age can be difficult at times but may also have advantages too, such as maintaining independence, greater mobility and a sense of purpose. However, a visit from someone who listens, and will perhaps wash up, can make all the difference to the day, even a life. Building friendships in this way is a possibility for all of us, whatever our age.

Allow conversations to gently unfold so that thoughts, feelings and ideas can arise naturally. If we are committed to a plan for our visit, we might block something new and wonderful from emerging in the moment; allow the unexpected.

Gathering interesting items, books, plants and so on as we go about our lives can be useful, especially if we regularly visit someone.

Creating a relaxed and warm environment is vital if we aspire to really connect. Lightness and humour can help build any relationship you are nurturing. You may be the only person ever to visit, or the only one seen that day; loneliness is an ever-increasing problem. It is indeed heart wrenching to hear the length of time some people spend alone.

It is worth being attentive as we go about our lives, noticing solitary people and offering help in any way we can. Our culture teaches us to be self-contained but, if we take that to its limit, the world will be a sad place. Certainty in life is an illusion, so is safety, but strong and resilient communities can be the root of creating a positive shift in society, one that will benefit everyone.

9. Gentle Preparations

To go in the dark with a light is to know the light,
To know the dark, go dark. Go without sight,
And find that the dark too blooms and sings
And is travelled by dark feet and dark wings.
– Wendell Berry

There are some beautiful preparations we can make for our dying, or that of another.

As I have already mentioned, my siblings and I sat around our dying mother's bed and sang through a repertoire of hymns she thought she might like at her funeral service. It appeared to give her comfort and reassurance. There was lightness and laughter and plenty of tea and cake. She also planned her readings. When the moment came, I found it easier knowing that this was her choice of farewell and exactly what she would have wanted. There are so many possibilities; some guidance can be helpful.

A friend ordered her willow coffin well in advance and when it arrived she found it so beautiful she kept it downstairs by the fire and enjoyed sitting in it in the evenings when she read the paper; that is, until the neighbours began to call – then it was hefted into the loft.

Perhaps a felt shroud is something that appeals, or a cardboard coffin. Either way, the top can be decorated with paintings, flowers or embroidery. Some people like to write poems, add photographs or tie ribbons or balloons. It can be fun, yes fun, to do this with friends in preparation for our own death or something that family and friends can take on as part of their shared grieving.

There is a much greater freedom than we might imagine around all aspects of death and dying. This is not a book about funerals but suffice it to say there are many that are, and I have added details of some of them at the end of the book. We do not have to go down the time-trodden route, even though undertakers can fulfil a very useful role. Increasingly, people are being drawn to a more 'do it yourself' approach that brings creativity and imagination into planning a ceremony. The result: something that is uniquely uplifting and memorable.

WILF AND JANE'S STORY – READY TOGETHER

Wilf and Jane were very companionable. They had shared a rich and varied life, one that began to reveal itself through their choices of music. They had travelled a long way to be cared for near their daughters – it appeared to be a very happy arrangement. We met weekly yet, despite my best efforts, only Wilf really engaged with my ideas. Jane would mostly snooze quietly on the sofa, one sleepy eye taking notice but otherwise she was quite content to do nothing – that is, until we got to music.

Wilf had sung in a choir in his youth and had a very distinguished voice, one he was surprisingly shy about sharing. However, he seemed to enjoy the makeshift efforts of our little singing group in the care home – in small doses. We sang the old wartime numbers and songs from the shows that everyone seemed to remember, and generally indulged in much laughter.

One quiet afternoon, as the sun streamed into the sitting room, we perched on the sofa like three old birds. We began to talk about musical favourites. I took out my phone, found the various pieces of music they mentioned and then played them. You can imagine their amazement. With increasing enthusiasm, they regaled me with anecdotes and stories relating to each song and sparkled with delight as they listened.

It was a highbrow list, which included Handel's *Zadok the Priest*, Franz Schubert's *Sonata for Violin and Piano No 1 in D Major*, Gregorio's *Allegri Miserere* and the hymn 'Dear Lord and Father of Mankind'. The list went on and so did the laughter, moments of humming and outbursts of song. We added to this fascinating selection week by week and I saved them as a playlist on my phone.

A compilation like this can be shared with the family or

care-home team, to be used in times of illness or confusion or even to play at the end of life as a comforting addition to palliative care. Wilf and Jane had shared with me an insightful and trusting glimpse into their life together and I felt truly honoured to have been the witness.

A playlist created for birthing is quite commonplace these days but what is less talked about is the value of a personal list of carefully chosen music to play at our dying.

REFLECTIONS ON WILF AND JANE'S STORY

By approaching some aspects of dying in simple and subtle ways it is possible to learn a bit more about what people's end-of-life wishes might be. Many people are reluctant to discuss this head-on. When there is hesitation about discussing the formal aspects, such as having a power of attorney or putting a DNR (do not resuscitate) form in place, creating situations like the one illustrated above may lightly open the door to other conversations that are less intense.

If one can drop some ideas about musical preferences into the time spent together, other thoughts may arise. Taken slowly and carefully, it can be surprising how much insight can be gleaned in this way.

Alternatively, this sort of activity can be pleasurable for its own sake. It could be a group activity, used to enhance the atmosphere of a lounge or day centre, with each person choosing some music they enjoy and thus building up a mutually beneficial compilation.

10. Ageing Gracefully and Enjoying It

It is the twilight zone between past and future
that is the precarious world of transformation...
– Marion Woodman

Ruth's story is the last story and is perhaps the most important one, especially if we aspire to a happy old age. It is certainly a good example of how joyful it can be if we prepare ourselves and our affairs in good time. If Ruth had an adage it might well have been Thoreau's 'simplify, simplify'.

From the moment I first met Ruth, she had a light-footed approach to her possessions. She enjoyed giving away anything she no longer found useful in her life, whether a table, chair, book, china or linen. If you hesitated, it was gone.

Our needs are generally so simple, yet we live in an age of clutter. As we age, we need even less, yet it often becomes harder to let things go. It also takes energy. However, our possessions can be a dubious legacy for those who come after us.

Always 'ahead of the game' and embracing the new, ageing became just another interesting phenomenon for Ruth, a challenge to learn from. Many lives were changed thanks to her curiosity and extraordinarily open approach to the new; she never closed her mind to anything, even her ageing and dying.

Long before we, her friends, felt she was ready, she determinedly sold up her little house and moved locally into sheltered housing. 'Plenty of time to really enjoy it,' she said. And she did! A new kitchen, fresh paint and carpets meant that Ruth loved her little flat to the full and never glanced back.

The layout was designed – of course – to ensure there was space for the ripple of visitors that trod the path to her door. We came, young and old, to drink tea and discuss universal concerns, along with matters of the heart. Sitting with Ruth was like resting by a refreshing stream; nothing contained her, yet she contained everything.

Ruth was a remarkable yoga teacher. She had taken it up at fifty years of age and taught for decades, latterly mostly to the other residents of her sheltered housing complex. Every week her companions would gather in the lounge and work (and laugh) through a series of exercises carefully designed to enhance mobility of both body and mind; 'flexible body, flexible mind' was her mantra.

And she ate well. Ruth understood the need to carefully tend her body so that it would continue to serve her to the end. 'Everything takes so much longer now,' she would mourn. 'When dressing up to go out I used to think, "this will wow them"; now I say to myself, "well that will have to do."'

Nothing in life is static. Even our own ageing bodies may become unrecognisable, but as the outer body ages so can the inner light shine brighter – as was certainly the case with Ruth. She read and studied all her life, cultivating her wisdom like a garden.

The day came when she knew it was time to move again, now into one room of her daughter's house. It was here that we massaged her with warm sesame oil and sat together watching her beloved birds feasting on seeds in the garden. It was here that finally, two days before she died, we held her hands and, along with Leonard Cohen, sang 'Hallelujah' – at full volume.

What a woman! I am sure she is singing still.

The Practical Pages

11. Retaining Physical Freedom

Every forest branch moves differently in the breeze
but as they sway, they connect at the roots.
– Rumi

Here are some simple and beautiful ways to encourage the body to move more freely.

The less we do the more we are inclined to take the easy option and remain seated. Getting back onto our feet again then becomes ever harder, even painful. Dear Ruth used to say, 'When you want to take the lift, take the stairs.' A good adage for all of us.

Connecting with the body by exercising helps us feel good about ourselves, and improves breathing, circulation and muscle tone. We may also find that sleep and appetite improve.

You do not have to be a professional to help people take up exercise but sometimes an outsider will have more success, especially when passivity has become ingrained. It is also more fun if you do it together, in chairs opposite each other perhaps.

All you need is a big welcoming smile, enthusiasm and a positive approach, plus a small towel rolled into a sausage shape that can be tucked in behind the small of the back. This allows the spine to ease back into its natural position and gives the lungs space to move. And some tennis balls. Yes, tennis balls are miracle workers! When rolled slowly and carefully around under bare feet, one at a time, they stimulate the reflexology points and keep the ankles flexible. It can be fun too and elicit laughter as they escape across the room.

With the spine now well supported, the breath is more likely to find its own rhythm. With a hand on the tummy, four fingers above the belly button, one can feel the ebb and flow of the breath as it settles. This area is known at the solar plexus, the sun centre, recognised by some disciplines as an important energy centre. It is useful to cultivate this quiet, conscious breathing as it is a helpful asset in times of anxiety, being calming and grounding. In and out, in and out, without strain or effort. Then breathe to the count of four – In 1 2 3 4, Out 1 2 3 4 – the reassuring hand still noticing the rise and fall of the tummy. Once this feels comfortable, try blowing out for as long as possible until you cannot speak, and then slowly in. This can be helpful for lowering blood pressure.

There are some easy stretches for when sitting upright on a chair (if possible; adapt if not; movement itself is so beneficial). With feet firmly placed upon the floor and hip width apart, we can take a breath in and slowly lift each arm in turn above the head, then lower it on the outbreath. Then clasp both hands and raise them on the inbreath as before, leaning slightly back when they are both up, before letting them down gently on an outbreath.

Two lovely little additions to this are that, when one arm is raised, we can bring it down on an outbreath to the opposite knee or ankle – a gentle, forward-bend twist that stimulates the inner organs as well as rotating the spine. Follow this by raising both arms, then bringing them down to the side of each ankle – a forward bend. That may be enough for one day.

If not – try this: a *sun and moon side stretch*. Sitting as before with the feet firmly planted, we exhale then breathe in as we take one arm up to the side and exhale as we take it over the head to the opposite side. Repeat both ways. Follow as before, taking both arms up and bending first one way then the other. As with all these moves, it is not about how far you can move but about enjoying the appointment with the body.

Now a *cat stretch* – sitting well positioned on a chair, place hands on the knees or thereabouts. First feel the base of the spine heavy and connected to the chair, breathe in and then arch the back as you breathe out, making a lovely curve, then as you breathe in again, reverse the movement and look up at the stars, letting the base of the spine rest deep on the chair and the lungs fill with air. This can be done two or three times, slowly and carefully, relishing the life-enhancing rhythm.

Now for the legs. Again, sitting solidly on the chair, allow the base of the spine to drop down and breathe in – on the exhalation, slowly lift first one leg then the other, keeping the lower leg relaxed and heavy. Repeat two or three times on each side. The breath is very helpful here. To begin with you may only manage to lift the leg an inch or two but, with practice, it will hopefully strengthen so that it is possible to move on to stage two. This entails straightening each leg in turn once it is raised, with a breath to separate one movement from the next. (It's easier to move into a position on the outbreath but please do not overconcern yourself about this.)

Now we are well into things and I am sure that, taken slowly and with laughter never far away, this exercise business will prove to be quite entertaining – remember there is no such thing as perfection in this game. Do not worry if you only manage one or two exercises per session, at least until the muscles have remembered what they are meant to do.

As we are gently moving round the body, we must not forget the feet, toes and ankles. This is easier without shoes or socks but again see how you go. Some people feel very exposed with bare feet, and self-conscious too – life does strange things to our feet, especially as we age. Spread the toes and try to lift and wiggle each one. This can be very funny and is rarely possible. Then lift each heel in turn, then the front of each foot – dropping the weight into the ground. If you push the feet away a little it is possible to rotate the ankles, first one way then the other – then spread the toes and screw them up into a ball once more. If standing, you can take the weight from one foot to the other to remind the body of its connection to the earth and of our place of balance.

Now, arms, hands and shoulders. Lift and rotate the shoulders, forward, up, back, up and down – slowly, slowly. Hold the hands out in front with the shoulders dropped and stretch, stretch, stretch those fingers wide, then clasp them tight. Back and forth several times. The wrists love being rotated too, both ways. In the past we used our arms and hands much more than we do now – think of wringing out wet clothes. Placing the hands together in the prayer position in front of the chest, we can press them together, which helps release fingers that are inclined to curl up as we age; then bring the clasped hands down towards the tummy button, up and down, slowly, slowly.

Finally, the head and neck. As you sit on the chair, consciously letting the weight of the spine drop into it, you will be creating space between each vertebra and able to feel the head's heaviness balanced on the spine. Give it a little wriggle. Then gently and slowly rotate the head, first one way then the other, always coming back to centre. Perhaps look up, then look down. Look over one shoulder, then the other – trying not to twist the whole body as you do so. Excellent!

With lots of reassurance, and lots of morale boosting, the results will speak for themselves.

12. Difficult Days

The heart that breaks open can contain the whole universe.
– Joanna Rogers Macy

'I should be dead.'

How often do we hear this unnerving statement? How on earth do we respond? There is no easy answer. It may trigger our own fears of dying and loss, leaving us devoid of words, shaken to our core. It is useful to disentangle these feelings.

Many of us will have had the experience of telling someone a deeply held fear or worry, only to have it dismissed or rejected. We are left feeling empty, even more alone and sometimes desperate. That precious pearl offered in a brave moment, trampled underfoot.

'You can't say that!' 'You mustn't say that!' 'Never say that again Dad, you know we love you.'

However, when truly heard, a flower can bloom in our hearts. Relief surges through us.

Allowing the words to settle, allowing the space to make way for more revelations or deeper conversations, can change everything. It might be a momentary feeling of despair, or perhaps something more fundamental that needs addressing. Discerning the difference is the challenge.

For most of us, our emotions waver even at the best of times; when we are chronically unwell, however, and have less to distract us, we are more susceptible to sinking into negativity. The refusal to acknowledge an unpalatable truth might shut the door, possibly forever; tragic if something else is bubbling under the surface waiting to be shared.

Instead, perhaps we might say, 'Goodness me! Is that how you are feeling today? That's tough,' or, 'Oh dear, can you tell me a bit more about that?' It can be a very lonely time if the world around us is unable to hear our truth – the restless murmurings of our heart.

Occasionally, the conditions that affect us when we age can be difficult to manage. The person in front of us may behave differently to the one we have known and loved. The boundaries and barriers that have sustained life to date have fallen away; the structure of manners and conventions are gone. Becoming rude, outspoken and occasionally physically challenging is not unusual, albeit painful to witness. Ideas relating to dressing and hygiene sometimes change; what mattered in the past is no longer of consequence. This can be confusing and distressing all round yet reinforces the need to have a power of attorney in place (see the next chapter) to ensure care can continue in a loving and respectful way, regardless of someone's state of mind. We never expect it to happen to us and it's a shock when it does.

Connecting with another in these situations can be complex; we may catch familiar moments of lucidity to draw upon, but fundamentally accepting that the person we know has slipped away is heartbreaking – a dying before the death. At some level, of course, they are still here, can hear everything and need to be loved and honoured regardless of the circumstances: grieving and loving in equal measure.

Professional help, along with carefully prescribed medication, can hold some symptoms in abeyance, along with conscious attempts to maintain warmth and kindness in our interactions. But, understandably, our own emotions can also flare up and overflow – fear, guilt, anger and resentment are not uncommon. For anyone in a caregiving role, being at a bedside 24/7 can feel draining, exhausting and, at times, utterly overwhelming; we feel forgotten and secluded from the world.

The warm, sometimes stifling, atmosphere of a sick room, the constant demands and lack of sleep may begin to take their toll. Admitting to our vulnerability, and accepting the help of outsiders, can become increasingly difficult the more exhausted we become. However, accepting our humanness is a good first step, as is taking a walk in a garden, a park or by running water, also speaking to a friend or health professional. Being outside in nature is always my first port of call when life is tough.

As friends or neighbours, it can be hard to know how and when to step in and help. Listening and acknowledging the difficulties is infinitely preferable to staying away. Our presence, whether as occasional minder, cleaner, shopper or purveyor of distractions and outings, will also be valuable.

An active and supportive community eases things for everyone. One of the most positive things we as individuals can do is to cultivate and engage our own.

13. Standing Strong, Initiating Conversations

We are blinding ourselves to the opportunity that exists
to change the individual experience of ageing for the better.
— *Being Mortal*, Atul Gawande

We owe it to ourselves and those we care for to have honest, clear conversations about how we want to spend our later years and to define our wishes around the end of life. We can say we don't care, we can say we don't want to think about it, but for sure, when it happens, and it can happen to any of us at any time, we will care and care passionately.

Initiating these conversations is vitally important, even if unwelcome. We are no longer children, afraid of stepping on the lines in case the bear will eat us. Talking about ageing and dying will not bring it towards us. As adults we have a responsibility to face up to the retort of 'that's too gloomy to talk about'; we have only to witness our friends and family go through unpleasant experiences to make us realise the importance of arranging these matters well in advance. This is particularly important if children are involved who need a guardian.

There is a file in my cupboard marked 'End of Life Stuff', where my family can access all my relevant paperwork, including passwords, important contacts and confidential details.

Technology has run rampant and medical procedures are available to keep us alive in a way that no one could have foreseen – and not always in the way we might wish. Without these conversations, matters can be taken out of our hands in complicated and sometimes tragic ways.

So – do try to find a way to talk about the subjects outlined below. Procedures can be put in place long before they might become a necessity. Note that there can be variations according to which part of the country you live in.

- **A power of attorney mandate.** It's a wise move to set up one of these in advance. It is a legally binding document that formally allocates people we trust to manage our affairs if we should lose capacity. There are two aspects: one concerns our health and welfare and the other our finances. Things can go badly wrong without the authority these documents give, especially in an emergency (making it perhaps impossible to finance care, as an example). Speak with those involved (and give them a copy) and with a solicitor, search online or follow links in the Reference Section at the back of this book.

- **A will:** this offers clarity and reduces confusion relating to the distribution of our effects after death. Again, speak with a solicitor or search online.

- **Advance decision:** this allows you to formally clarify any treatments you don't want in the future in case you lose capacity and are unable to communicate your wishes yourself. When signed and witnessed this is a legally binding document. For more information, search online or follow the links in the Reference Section at the back of the book. I also suggest giving copies to close family, your GP and those who will be involved with your care.

- **A do not resuscitate (DNR) form**, if this is your choice. Paramedics are duty bound to attempt resuscitation regardless of age or stage in life if called in an emergency, unless there are contrary indications. For some people, resuscitation will not be welcome. It could be uncomfortable or could delay or prevent what might have been a peaceful dying. Easily recognisable, it is helpful to have this form by the door or at the top of the file of medical records when tending an ageing or dying person. Surgeries do have pamphlets that detail the facts, both positive and negative, but in my experience, you need to ask for them. As when we become an organ donor, it is important to discuss this with family or those who might be involved in your care.

Once our own affairs are in order, we can approach our ageing and dying with a lighter step and then perhaps help others to do so too. In the past, people were not encouraged to think about these things, nor was it quite so important or easy. How we respond to life's challenges ripples down the generations. We can choose our legacy.

14. What to Expect When Someone Is Dying

> When you find you are dying – keep it like the prized
> possession it is.
> – *Die Wise*, Stephen Jenkinson

There is no rehearsal for dying. As in birthing, no manual prepares us for the actual experience. Whether as the dying person or as the companion on the way, our general lack of familiarity with death can make this feel like unknown territory.

There will probably be raw emotions about, unexpected reactions from family and friends or perhaps unresolved differences erupting, all exacerbated by exhaustion. At other times, there is an acceptance and peace and an atmosphere of deep serenity. It is not unusual to be struck by a different feeling in the room, not only thanks to your careful efforts to make it calm and beautiful but also owing to some other undefined quality, which is hard to describe yet not easily forgotten.

In the preceding days or weeks, you may have noticed a withdrawal in the person you are accompanying. Maybe an emergence or re-emergence of a spiritual awareness, a need for conversations around belief or afterlife. This time can be one of great transformation. It is important to acknowledge this and not to set up barriers to what seems real to them or impose one's own ideas.

Your friend may be less interested in the happenings around them, have less interest in food or only want to sleep. It can be our instinct to encourage someone to eat because we know that it sustains life. However, daring to be honest and accepting that this is a gently unfolding process of letting go can save much distress for all concerned.

It is not unusual for someone at this stage of the dying process to gaze into the distance or seem to be conversing with unseen people. It is easy to dismiss this and get upset. However, once again it's important not to brush it aside, or to negate it. Who are we to know the truth of the moment?

To be with someone at this time can be an enormous privilege, and quite a responsibility too. It is an opportunity that does not come often. It may also be tough, possibly long and both emotionally and physically draining. Support is valuable. We might also witness the 'crowning' of a life, something that touches the essence of everything that has ever mattered. It is possible to be fundamentally changed by the experience.

From now on in, there is no hiding, no more game-playing or comfortable charades to act out. It is also never too late for remarkable happenings, extraordinary conversations and healings, even at the bedside. Ancestral feuds, previously unspoken secrets and well-rehearsed resentments can be resolved, releasing years of carried pain and giving future generations an unhampered future, a cleaner slate on which to make their own mark. There is great power in forgiveness.

It's worth remembering that unresolved situations and

difficult relationships sometimes prevent one from letting go. Be attentive to a 'holding on with purpose' feeling – when someone is clearly ready to die but cannot for some reason slip out and away. Maybe they feel formal absolution is needed for something they have done or said: careful and intuitive questioning may discern what is needed and who is best to offer this forgiveness – a spiritual authority or a respected friend? Often, reassurance, gentle enquiry and following our own instinct can be enough.

Homeopathy, acupuncture and the use of Bach flower remedies can all prove very helpful for everyone involved in end-of-life care. Contact a competent practitioner who can support your personal needs. Links are at the back of the book.

Dying can be hard work. It might be important to protect the dying person from disturbances and inappropriate visitors. A little teddy tucked into the crook of the arm can be a comfort, especially if you need to absent yourself for a while. Also, the fragrance of lavender oil on the pillow, soft music playing or, for some, the radio. This stage of the dying process can resemble a birth in reverse and take a while, possibly setting up an emotional strain for some as life continues apace outside. Having some knitting to hand, a paper to read or other peaceful activities for you to do are normalising for everyone – friendly, familiar and comforting. Again, remember how it was when we were ill as children.

Sometimes people need reassurance that it's OK to die – to leave those who love them. They may need to be told that although they will be missed, they will not be forgotten and will always be loved: 'Mum, it's really OK for you to go. We will be very, very sad but we can manage now. It's your time.' It is like giving permission. The relief can sometimes be instantaneous.

Sharing kindly stories that honour the moment is also fine.

Sitting with a dying person and airing grievances or sorting disagreements, however, should be undertaken in another room. The one you know, and love, is still very much here, even if you no longer recognise them. Talk to them, sing to them, croon and remember old lullabies. Hearing is apparently the last sense to leave.

Reading aloud from carefully chosen books, maybe biblical texts, prayers or gentle tales such as *The Snowflake* by Paul Gallico or passages from *Benedictus* by John O' Donohue, can be a lovely thing to do, especially as consciousness comes and goes, as can lightly touching the feet, stroking the hair, freshening the face or holding the hands. These gestures are calming and grounding for both the dying person and those who are in attendance. The time will come, however, when it is probably best to stand by and just witness. Anything else is a distraction from the sometimes arduous journey being enacted before us. Presence is the most valuable gift, and all that is needed.

Please note: no candles must be burning when oxygen is in use.

15. Signs of Dying

Here rolls the sea
And even here
Lies the other shore
Waiting to be reached
Yes, here is the everlasting present
Not distant
Not anywhere else.
– Rabindranath Tagore

Dying is a process. Each death is unique. Although there are no certainties, it can be helpful to have some idea as to what you might expect.

You will probably be working alongside medical professionals, hospice nurses or a care team but do not underestimate the power of your presence.

- Ensure the wishes of your friend are met, that the room is not only warm, welcoming and smells fresh, but has that special atmosphere about it that only you can create – calm, loving and peaceful.

- Matching your breath with that of your friend, if it's not too extreme, can feel supportive. Sitting quietly and just breathing in when they breathe in and breathing out as they breathe out is simple and beautiful.

- Cheyne–Stokes is the name given to a loud, sometimes discordant, type of breathing that can happen at this time and is not one you should try to match. It can occur towards the end and is nothing to be alarmed about. If in doubt, mention it to your medical support.

- Continue to reassure, encourage and offer affirmations of love and approval. Remember the person you are accompanying may be aware of his/her surroundings and all that is being said.

- The lessening of appetite as the body begins to shut down is quite normal. You can be supportive by ensuring they are not pressured to eat.

- Lightly sponging the lips and mouth helps to keep them soft and hydrated, especially when liquids are no longer being drunk. There are special sponges that can make it easier. Ask your medical support about this.

- As the digestion slows, so may continence become affected. Your medical professional will help you with this.

- You may notice an unusual, very particular and hard-to-describe smell about the person as the metabolic system slows toward the end – this is quite normal.

- There will be increasing detachment from the immediate surroundings. Perhaps a staring into the distance or words spoken to someone beyond our vision. Also, more sleepiness and increasing spells of quiet.

- The person's language may change; references to going home, leaving or being collected are not uncommon.

- A level of agitation is quite normal and may have various causes – perhaps speak to your medical professional. Repetitive picking at the covers often indicates the end is near.

- The skin changes colour, sometimes with a flush, and then becomes opaque or grey. The nails of toes and fingers become pale or blue and may be cool to the touch.

- As indicated in the chapters above, peaceful music, low lighting, essential oils in a burner (eucalyptus, lemon, cedarwood and cypress are all good), kindly conversation and gentle reminiscing all contribute to a calm and loving atmosphere.

- There can be a last-minute flare-up of vitality: the dying person may sit up, demand food or ask to see a certain friend or relative. This will probably be followed by a resting back and a steady fading.

- Moisture can gather in the throat, precipitating a cough or rattle towards the end.

- The breath often stops before the heart.

- It can be hard to know the exact moment of death. Perhaps there is a sense that something has shifted, that something quite tangible has left. The skin may look different as the colour fades. Each departure is different.

- There is no rush when death occurs. Breathing has stopped, the world has changed, nothing will ever be the same again. It is worth taking a moment to sit, pause and just be. Take your time.

- It is, however, important to note the time of death as accurately as possible.

- Some people choose to open the window, blow out the candle, go quickly to inform others and set in motion the preparations for burial – there is no right or wrong.

- Alternatively, we can continue the vigil, or enact a ceremony if this is our choice or culture – to hold the world at bay until it feels right to move on to the practical details. There is no rush. Some people like to sit for a few hours, or even days. Again, there is no 'normal' in death.

- Some care homes, hospitals and hospices have a special room set aside for families to visit or sit with the resting body. In Scotland, it will probably be the front room where the body is viewed and grieved over by the family and community.

- Washing and anointing the body can be a beautiful honouring of a life, whether undertaken alone or with others. Traditionally, families were expected to take on this role, never considering for one moment passing it on to someone else. Nowadays, it is more often done by nurses or funeral directors. Our experience in these matters has sadly been forgotten. However, we can still do it ourselves.

WASHING THE BODY

If this is something you choose to do, take heart. It is very simple and very beautiful. There are no rules – you can take your time and make it what you want, a truly lovely thing to do for someone you care for. A chance to make your final farewell, show your love and perhaps share your grief, if undertaken with others.

- Taking a bowl of warm water, fresh towels and essential oils of your choice (geranium, lavender, rose…), work round the body, tenderly and respectfully washing and drying each limb, blessing and offering gratitude to each part. For instance: 'I thank and bless this hand for all it has held, loved and cradled', 'I bless and thank this foot for each step it has taken in this life.'

- For some there are songs, lullabies or chants to sing. For others it is a time of quiet reflection, undertaken in silence.

- At the head, take a clean cloth, refresh the water and take time to wipe or sponge it with care, as you might have done in life; go around the eyes, mouth, jaw and hairline.

- Anointing the body with special oil can be a beautiful ceremonial act; pick a spot on the brow, solar plexus, the palms of the hands or the soles of the feet, or a light application over the whole body using a base oil, like almond, with the oil of your choice. Frankincense might be one, sandalwood another and rose is equally lovely. It's worth spending a little time if you can, finding those that you like. Lavender is the only oil that is safe to use undiluted.

- This simple ceremony can be a very helpful and beautiful way of saying goodbye and expressing grief.

This little book does not cover the time after death. Funerals and all that goes with them are a subject unto themselves. There are some ideas and links at the back of the book that may prove helpful. Suffice it to say that there is much greater freedom to do what feels right at the time than we perhaps expect.

16. We Grieve Each Passing

> I did not know what to say to him. I felt awkward and
> blundering.
> I did not know how I could reach him, where I could overtake
> him and go on hand in hand with him once more.
> It's such a secret place, the land of tears.
> – *The Little Prince*, Antoine de Saint-Exupéry

Life is rich with endings. We are given endless opportunities to practise before the final letting go. Autumn makes way for winter; spring returns each year. Children leave home, jobs change, one house move follows another and seasons come and go. Every farewell is a small dying, every change in circumstance and stage of life requires a closure of one kind or another. Then we too grow old.

Endings are also beginnings; every plant emerges from the compost of the old – we are irrevocably intertwined with all that is. Grieving is a fundamental part of being alive, but is rarely acknowledged for the vitally important process it is. It is one that has no clear path yet needs to be travelled with as much courage as we can muster. It's mostly undertaken alone. Our culture expects us to 'get over it' promptly and return to our role in the world after a painfully brief bereavement leave

– it's more convenient that way, less messy. But sorrow cannot be bargained with. The heart has its own process.

It is well documented that animals cry in their grief, that they truly mourn their companions and feel emotions just like us. To respond to a death as many of us would dearly love to do might be considered quite scary – an out-of-control response. However, no one judges the elephant that stamps and howls for days, or a swan that grieves around the nest.

Some care establishments have a policy of total dissociation from the deaths of their residents. Following a death, the dead body is removed while everyone is at lunch and the curtains are inexplicably drawn. Thereafter, no one mentions the death again except in whispers. It is no wonder that fear builds up. Having a small memorial table in the hallway, with a photograph, poem, battery-powered candle and a posy of flowers, ensures that everyone is aware of the shift in energy – there has been a death and there can be a grieving, collective or individual.

Taking time, making time and allowing feelings to be what they are is important. Being around those who understand, spending time alone if that's your way, acknowledging what you need with honesty and sincerity all pave the way towards a new kind of wholeness. No one will know exactly what is best for you except you. There is no rush.

For those who are overwhelmed, there are organisations which can offer help (see the links at the back of the book). It's good to sleep lots, eat well and be out in nature as much as possible: reading, dancing, drumming, wild swimming or sitting out on hilltops with the wind. There is something essentially comforting about being in nature. She's seen it all before and can show us the way. Take time to listen. Take time to breathe and find your own rhythm again.

Sadly, there are no shortcuts, but kind and loving friends and family can make a difference, as can a strong community, both of which are sorely lacking for some. Individually, we must look out for each other – there is nothing like being able to share our sorrow with a friendly other.

'All shall be well, and all manner of thing shall be well.' Wise words by Dame Julian of Norwich.

17. The Way Forward

Our reverence for independence takes no account of the reality
of what happens in later life: sooner or later independence will
be impossible.
— *Being Mortal*, Atul Gawande

This small volume is my contribution to experiencing ageing
and dying with an expanded understanding, bringing the truth
of a finite existence into our everyday reality and allowing it to
enhance our living.

Waking up to our mortality is fundamental to our existence.

Life as we know it is on the brink of fundamental change
as global warming becomes a climate crisis – an increasingly
unavoidable reality – and so we must rouse ourselves from
the stupor of denial and look the possibility of a vastly altered
future in the eye. Apparently, there is not much time.

Grief is all around us – witnessing the daily extinction of
species is the most heartbreaking experience.

We can, however, be part of an extraordinary renaissance
in how we approach these issues – the choices we make,
conversations we have and actions we take. By collectively
harnessing our energies, we can create a new paradigm for
ageing and dying, and not before time.

It is a missed opportunity to sit on the sidelines and expect it all to happen without us. Contributing keeps us alert, interesting and useful. There is so much potential alongside the tragedy. We can imagine the unimaginable – a new future not only personally but also globally.

Celebrating the later stages of life and preparing carefully for the inevitable is a process we can come to appreciate, not run from. Future generations will learn from us as we learn from those who came before us.

We all need wise people to turn to, whatever our age. Never more so than now with the world in such turmoil. Elderhood is not a default – we must learn it and earn it.

The natural world offers endless examples of exquisite full-blooded living and dying. My belief is that if we can get out there and participate in it, alone or with others, our lives will be the richer.

Finally, I hope the stories illustrated here will offer useful insights and be helpful in whatever role you carry in this life. And remember, you are not alone. Ageing and dying are universal experiences: we all do them for the first time.

Let us support and encourage each other, welcome the inevitable and find humour in the difficulties. Good luck and thank you for travelling with me thus far.

Further Reading and Guidance Notes

BOOKS

- *Die Wise, A Manifesto for Sanity and Soul*, Stephen Jenkinson

- *The End of Life Namaste Care Program for People with Dementia*, Joyce Simard

- *The Five Invitations: Discovering What Death Can Teach Us About Living Fully*, Frank Ostaseski

- *Intimate Death: How the Dying Teach us to Live*, Marie de Hennezel

- *The Soul Midwife's Handbook: The Holistic and Spiritual Care of the Dying*, Felicity Warner

- *Being Mortal: Illness, Medicine, and What Matters at the End*, Atul Gawande

- *A Life Worth Living – How Someone You Love Can Still Enjoy Life in a Nursing Home*, William H. Thomas, MD

- *When Breath Becomes Air: What Makes Life Worth Living in the Face of Death?* Paul Kalanithi

- *What Dementia Teaches Us About Love*, Nicci Gerrard
- *Contented Dementia*, Oliver James
- *How to Have a Good Death*, Esther Rantzen
- *End of Life Care: A Guide for Therapists, Artists and Art Therapists*, Nigel Hartley
- *No Death No Fear*, Thich Nhat Hanh
- *A Scattering*, Christopher Reid
- *The Creative Arts in Palliative Care*, Nigel Hartley
- *Sacred Dying, Creating Rituals for Embracing the End of Life*, Megory Anderson
- *Who Dies*, Stephen Levine
- *Grief is The Thing with Feathers*, Max Porter
- *The Built Moment*, Lavinia Greenlaw
- *Being with Dying*, Joan Halifax
- *With the End in Mind, Death: Dying and Wisdom in an Age of Denial*, Kathryn Mannix
- *Transforming the Quality of Life for People with Dementia through Contact with the Natural World*, edited by Jane Gilliard and Mary Marshall

FILMS

- *Griefwalker* – A film by Stephen Jenkinson that offers a fresh approach to dying. A free download from the Canadian Film Board. https://www.nfb.ca/film/griefwalker/
- *Patch Adams* – The true story of Patch Adams, a clown

doctor, and his (at the time) revolutionary approach to person-centred care in hospitals and hospices.

- *Departures* – The extraordinary story of a Japanese cellist who finds himself learning the detailed skills of a mortician when his orchestra is disbanded.

- *The Diving Bell and the Butterfly* – The true story of the 43-year-old editor of *Elle*magazine who, after suffering a massive stroke, was found to have locked-in syndrome.

ADVANCE DIRECTIVES/LIVING WILLS

- https://compassionindying.org.uk/library/advance-directives-living-wills-scotland/

- https://compassionindying.org.uk/library/advance-decision-pack/

CONVERSATIONS

- https://compassionindying.org.uk/library/starting-the-conversation/

- http://www.nairncab.org.uk/projects/taking-control-illness-and-dying/

- https://www.goodlifedeathgrief.org.uk/

CARERS' SUPPORT

- https://www.mariecurie.org.uk/

- https://www.macmillan.org.uk/about-us

- www.dementiauk.org.org/the-use-of-dolls-in-dementia-care/

DOULAS/SOUL MIDWIVES

- https://www.lwdwtraining.uk
- http://www.soulmidwives.co.uk/
- https://eol-doula.uk

HOSPICES

- www.stchristophers.org.uk
- https://www.chas.org.uk/
- https://www.hospiceuk.org/

END-OF-LIFE SUPPORT

- Centre for Death and Society, Bath. CDAS – www.bath.ac.uk

- Namaste Care – www.namastecare.com

- www.whatmattersnow.org – a very useful site that allows the carer/cared-for person to update friends and family (or anyone they select) to keep in touch and know what/when/ how to be of help/visit and what gifts will be most appreciated. This can be invaluable.

- Dignity in Dying – www.dignityindying.org.uk

- Simeon Care – personalised, Rudolph Steiner-based care home – www.simeoncare.org

- Scottish Partnership for Palliative Care – www.palliativecarescotland.org

- Alzheimer's Society – Alzheimers.org.uk

BODY PREPARATION

- Pushing up the Daisies – Bringing Death Home, www.pushingupthedaisies.org.uk

- Coffins: Willow – by Karen Collins via Naturally Useful, www.naturallyuseful.co.uk

- Shrouds – exquisite leaf cocoons in handmade felt, www.bellacouche.com

FUNERALS

- http://www.naturaldeath.org.uk/

- http://www.greenfuse.co.uk

- The Dead Good Funerals Guide – www.deadgoodguides.com

NATURE CONNECTION

- Wild Wise: Call to the Wild – provides the inspiration for all ages to become connected to the wonder and enchantment of the natural world, www.wildwise.co.uk

- Landworks – a groundbreaking training scheme for offenders that supports rehabilitation through work mostly on the land, www.landworks.ork.uk

- Embercombe – Inspired by nature, self-development programmes for all ages to reconnect with the wild, authentic self, www.embercombe.org

- Forest Schools – nature-based communities where trained practitioners nurture learning and discovery for young people, www.forestschools.com

OTHER

- https://hpathy.com/homeopathy-papers/the-end-of-life-and-homeopathy/
- www.bachcentre.com/centre/remedies.htm

Acknowledgements

Grateful thanks to all the extraordinary and wonderful people who have helped bring *Leaves of Love* to publication, especially the best support team imaginable, George, Emma, Bertie, Kate and Rose, my children.

Also, my long-suffering friends, who have stood by me, listened to me read and reread this manuscript, patiently, kindly, carefully and sometimes more times than they would have perhaps liked. Others printed my illustrations, filmed films and offered suggestions or valuable leads, without which there would have been no book. Thank you.

Then my crowdfunding supporters – every single hard-earned penny has come from friends and strangers who believed in the importance of this project. I have been stunned by your generosity – thank you all.

I cannot overlook this opportunity to thank some key guides who have immeasurably influenced my life and the direction it has taken:

Hermione Elliot of Living Well Dying Well laid down the bones of being an end-of-life doula, a role that was fleshed out by the privilege, tenderness and love that has encompassed the many shared experiences at the hearthstone of life and death.

Chris Salisbury of Wild Wise who, from his sunny perch in Devon, offered me exactly what I needed when I needed it – an immersion in nature.

Stephen Jenkinson, whose visionary approach to dying encouraged and inspired me to trust my own instinctual feelings about approaching and being with our dying ones. His book *Die Wise* and film *Griefwalker* have been wonderful companions on the way.

Bill Plotkin, for writing *Soulcraft* and *Wild Mind*, without which I would never have sat in the desert, learned the majesty of mystery and be where I am now. I deeply value his continued wisdom and presence in my life as well as that of my guide, Sage Magdalen.

Geneen Haagen showed me what was right in front of my eyes, a path of truth that only I could follow. Her unique insights and writings, with their startling clarity and beauty, continue to remind me of what is possible.

Martin Shaw of the West Country School of Myth and Storytelling unveiled the storyteller in me, without which I would not have been able to execute my vision.

Jeremy Whitehorn, for listening to a stranger, sharing his insights and sometimes ruthlessly reminding me of how to deliver my best. Trusting in me at the outset of this whole journey was the most extraordinary gift he could have offered.

Lastly, but most importantly, there are the story makers and their families, without whom I could not have written these pages. Their families' trust in me and willingness to have their stories shared, even with complete upside-down anonymity, has been a leap of faith and kindness. Blessings on you.

CREDITS FOR EPIGRAPHS

Introduction: 'The Way It Is' from *Ask Me: 100 Essential Poems*. ©*1977, (Placeholder 1) 2014* © William Stafford and the Estate of William Stafford, reprinted with the permission of The Permissions Co. LLC. On behalf of Graywolf Press, Minneapolis, Minnesota.

2: *The Tibetan Book of Living and Dying* by Soghal Rinpoche. Published by Rider. Reproduced by permission of the Random House Group Ltd © 2008.

5: Attributed to John Muir. Use acknowledged and approved by Isabelle Miller at John Muir Centre, Pitlochry.

6: Extract from an interview with George Sylvester Viereck in *The Saturday Evening Post*, 26 October 1929. Permission granted for inclusion here by the Albert Einstein archives, the Hebrew University of Jerusalem.

8: Krishnamurti, *Letters to Schools,* Gollancz.

9: Extract from *Farming – A Handbook*, by Wendell Berry. Publisher: HardcourtBrace Jovanovic, 1967. Reproduced by kind permission of the author.

10: Extract from *The Pregnant Virgin: a process of Psychological Transformation*, Marion Woodman, 1985. Published by Innercity Books. Permission granted for use here by Scott Milligen of Innercity Books.

12: Excerpt from *Pass it on: Five stories that can change the world* by Joanna Macy. Permission granted for use by Parallax Press, parallax.org.

13 & 17: Extract from *Being Mortal* by Atul Gawande, Profile Books Ltd, 2015 pp35 & 22. Reproduced in accordance with fair usage (Penny Daniel, Rights Director at Profile Books).

14: Extract from *Die Wise: A Manifesto for Sanity and Soul* by Stephen Jenkinson. Published by North Atlantic Books, © 2015. Reprinted here with permission from North Atlantic Books.

16: Extract from *The Little Prince*, by Antoine de Saint-Exupéry. Published by Pan Books in association with William Heinemann Ltd, 1974.

Unbound is the world's first crowdfunding publisher, established in 2011.

We believe that wonderful things can happen when you clear a path for people who share a passion. That's why we've built a platform that brings together readers and authors to crowdfund books they believe in – and give fresh ideas that don't fit the traditional mould the chance they deserve.

This book is in your hands because readers made it possible. Everyone who pledged their support is listed at the front of the book and below. Join them by visiting unbound.com and supporting a book today.

Elizabeth Susan Armstrong
Sarah Ashton
Colleen Bain
Margery Bambrick
Val Bayliss-Brideaux
Becky Bolton
Justin Bonnet
Zélia Bowles
Tom Carr-Ellison
Dot Cato
Ruth Chadwick
Fiona Cornish
Elspeth Crichton Stuart
Tessa Cumming-Bruce
Kate Darrah
Gail Davidson
Chloe Deakin
Catherine Delamain
Glenn Dietz

Emma Dixon
Allie Dolan
Erica
Linda Everitt
Christina Fanshawe
Lainy Farmer
Chris Fenn
Yvonne Flett
Felicity Forrest
Linda Fox
Susanne Frank
Louise Gardner
Jo Gibb
Sally Gouldstone
Kate Gouzes
Diana Greene
Wilma Harris
Pamela Ingleby
Emmy Maddy Johnston

Laura Jump
Dolly Kary
Dan Kieran
Helene Kreysa
Lisa Lawson
Joanne Legge
Diana Lindon
Sandra Ling
Becky Logan
Gillian Lowe
Helen Lunn
Rudi Magrix
Kirsten Maguire
Joan Mann
Barbara Joan Meier
Sayoko Meyer
Stephanie Mitchell
John Mitchinson
Rosalie Monod de Froideville
Helen Muir
Carlo Navato
Mary Nelson
Laura Newbury
Claire Newman
Morven Paterson
Kate Peros
Alessandro Pierfederici
Justin Pollard
Leonie Laya Poortvliet
Anna Raven

Camilla Revell
Philip Revell
Patricia Robertson
Neil Robson
John Ross
Lorraine Ross
B S
Barbara Schofield
Eva Schonveld
Mooie Scott
Laurence Shapiro
Nancy G Shapiro
Gayano Shaw
George & Parry Shirey
Jerry Simcock
Chris Simmonds
Alexandra Simmons
Louise Simmons
Rebecca Skillman
Lesley Smith
Wendy Staden
Elspeth Strohm
Nicky Swan
Christina Turley
Teresa Verney
Victoria Whitehouse
Catherine Williamson
Elisabeth Wilson
Anna Wimbledon